Pr

Life,

"BSavvy is always a candid refreshing experience. Having read many of her poems I have come to identify her ink as pure, classy and full of romantic hope and energy. She writes with a smile in that her work is always transparent of her true motions. I get the feeling that the beauty in her words matches the beauty in her heart and spirit and bridges the readers to her pen in a way that only she can do."--- Steve McGoy aka SCORPIO SESSIONS

"Reading BSavvy's art (poetry) is an instant vacation. It's so pleasant and vivid, it'll leave you craving more, and you'll find yourself reading again and again for the rare joy and love and wisdom it blesses the heart and soul with. With every read, it engages you and places your heart and mind in a place that will leave you speechless."---Tavares Jones

"BSavvy's Poetry conveys a message of Love, Life, and all its lessons in between. She touches the heart & soul with a spiritually realistic, open-minded approach. You will always find yourself either reflecting deeply, smiling, or sighing from beautifully written touches of a Lovely & Wonderful Poetess." ---Mavrick

New York

Published by ZLOVE a ZLS Publishing Imprint.

Visit the authors website at: http://www.bsavvypoetry.com/

Cover Design by Vann Taylor
Interior Book Designed by Lishone' Bowsky
Ebook Designed by ZLS Publishing
10 9 8 7 6 5 4 3 2 1

ISBN 978-0-9845986-5-6
Library of Congress Control Number: 2012949971

This Book is dedicated to my daughter Savannah Green. Mommy loves you and remember baby girl, the sky is the limit so never stop reaching for the stars

Love

Table of Contents

Part I: Life

Table of Contents

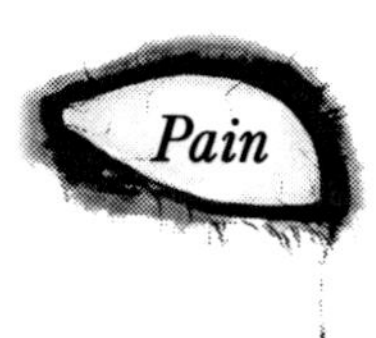

Table of Contents

LIFE

Life, Love & Pain

Blows from the storms
Boat just rocking
From the waves
It crashes hard
Trials
&
Tribulations
You just can't seem to stop

Learning and giving
Moving from selfish to selfless
Floating on cloud nine
Feelings of ecstasy
Laughter replaces pain

Then love is gone
Leaving you in the end
With nothing, but pain
Scared to love again
Life's just too hard
Feelings of dejection
Hurt
&
Rage
With wounds you wish would just heal already

Life, Love & Pain

When it all boils down to it
Isn't this all we have in the end
Life
    Love
        &
         Pain

When the cycle is over
It just repeats itself again

My Lines

Lines written revealing
Private thoughts
Secret hurts
Love gained
To
Love lost

Metaphors describing
Feelings
Situations
Pains
The inner struggle
The inner turmoil

You call it poetry
For me I'm just writing
Cause that's what I do
To release all that lies inside of me

Revealing myself little by little
To those that I don't know
Hoping they can relate
Hoping I can help encourage someone else
Along my way

Knowing if I made it this far
Despite the many knock downs
So can you

Knowing that after I release
and get up from my PC
I can feel a little lighter

Dreams and secret wishes
I jot down
Knowing one day
What I dream
Will be my reality

Discouragement hits hard
Sometimes I can be my worst critic
And
Though I show cool and calm
On the surface
People just don't know the inner turmoil

The anxiety attacks
I battle every single day and night
But
I know God is with me
Even if there's no one else
I can lean on

So at night I talk to Him
Let him hear my struggle
And knowing he can decipher my moans

And my tears
I know he caught each
And
Every one of them

So for me
I have to write
If not I think
I would have gone 730

My lines
My words
My release

And there in lies my inner healing
My inner peace

My pen
My paper
I need them

Journey

On my journey of self discovery
Taking time to analyze self
Understanding
That everything stems from your childhood experience
And as you grow
Your shoulders get heavy
          Because
You pick up more baggage along your way

Have many masks
          But
Lately I can't seem to find any of them
I'm open
Transparent
Leaving me constantly vulnerable
This is such a new experience
But they say
It's because
You're on a way to a healing

It's painful on this journey
Realizations hit hard
Things you never realized now come to light
Tears that I don't like to shed
Are constantly trying to make its way down
So I am fighting against myself
So this time I learn to let them fall
For it doesn't make me weak
          But

Reminding me
That I am human overall
And it's a way for the self to release
Many years of pent up emotions
It's the only way I can truly heal

So quick to blame others
When in reality people only irritate you
Or make you mad
Because they are stimulating something already in you
Perhaps your weakness you try to hide
Perhaps they resemble someone that did you bad

Two fingers pointing at them
But
Three should be pointing back at you
For its not them
In reality it's you

Learning more and more about attraction
&
The fact you attract certain people
Because of something in you

People do come in your life for a reason
Sometimes those difficult people
Are there to help you grow
And when you learn the lesson
You pass go
You move on to the next level
Which means time to let that person go

I have a long way to go
But I'm determined to heal and grow
And if that means while I'm on my journey
If I have to leave people
Then that's just what I have to do
Can't afford for anyone to stunt my growth

And

Perhaps face the fact
That just maybe
I am suppose to be alone
And maybe that is one of life lessons
I have to learn
Who knows

Got a box full of tissues
And some music to play in the background
With a glass of wine in my hand

While I read
While I dig
While I reflect
Over my life

Starting with my childhood
And comforting that little girl
Giving her something she never had

A shoulder to cry on
A trusted soul to lean on
A protector and a friend

My mission right now
Is to heal her
So I can be that great woman now
Fully balanced
Totally rounded
With no need for a mask
Because
I trust life and its process
And know in the end
I'll be just fine
And a better me
Then when I first started on my journey

A Sunrise Kiss

Curled up under the covers
Slight breeze coming in
All is still
        &
It's quiet around me
Just my own thoughts running rampant in my head

Rolling over
Eyes still closed shut
Don't really want to get up
Want to sleep on and on forever

Breathing in…
Breathing out...

Hair falling in front of my face
Gently sweeping it over
Putting my hand back under the covers
Then grabbing my pillow
        &
Hugging it tight

Feeling calmness slowing taking over
As I paint pictures in my mind
Letting my imagination soar
And smiling

And it kissed me
Good morning
And I just smiled

And as I slowly open my eyes
I see the sun rise
And it kissed me
Good morning
And I just smiled

Cruisin'

There I was crusin down I95
Wind hitting my face
Blowing my hair around
Music pumping
Fingers snapping
Not a care in the world

I'm just driving
Wishing this car could take me further
End up somewhere
Perhaps another town
Another city
Willing to just explore

I'm crusin down I95
Fell in love again
Found back my first love
My music
You see
For it soothes me
Takes me away

I'm singing
I'm snapping
I'm bopping my head
Just feeling so darn good
Wind blowing
Sun shinning
Just driving

Cars driving by
Wondering wassup with her?
I just smile
Then wink my eye
Little do they know
I'm just enjoying my own company

I'm crusin down I95
See my exit
Dang!
I hate to have to get off
Something takes a hold of me
I end up gunning it
Went right past my exit

That's just fine with me
I'm enjoying my first love
My music
I'm singing again
Thought I lost my voice
But, nope I got it back

I'm snapping
I'm smiling
I'm singing
I'm bopping
To the beat
It's flowing through me
I don't want to stop driving

Just escape in my music
And re-create my life
Just by listening to it
Erase the bad memories
Replace it with some good ones
My smile is contagious

I'm just crusin down I95

6

Day Dreaming

Packing my bag
Going to board a flight
Non – stop to Jamaica

Checking in to the hotel

Got the keys to my room
Place my bags down on the ground
Taking in my surroundings

In search for the bar
Needing me a drink right about now

Oohh that hit the spot
Need to tell the bartender
I want another round

Starting to unwind
Feeling good inside
Nothing bothering me
I'm just smiling

Hmm!
Think I will hit the beach
Let me go and put on the bikini

Listening to my love songs
Staring out into the ocean
With my drink in my hand

Ahh!
Look at that couple
Makes me a little jealous
They have what I don't have
They have each other

Attention goes back to the water
Admiring how the water has no beginning and no end
It just keeps going

Feeling the warm breeze
Sun shining bright
But, far from humid
I'm loving it

This is just what the dr. ordered

Feel the stress starting to lessen
I'm exhaling

I'm feeling good right about now

Think I want to take a dip

Floating on my back
Staring up at the sky
I love to do this
Helps to block everyone out
Just me and my thoughts

The good thoughts
It's just so soothing

BSavvy

Getting out the water
Go back and lay down
Pushing thoughts
That don't coincide with what I'm feeling to the side

Can't be bothered right now

I'm day dreaming
Of where I want to be right now

That's on the beach in Jamaica with a drink in my hand

Going With the Flow

Just going with the flow of life
Riding the waves
Taking the hits from the under currents
Then sailing on the calm seas
        To
Basking in the rays
That shine and makes the waters glisten

Just going with the flow

Sailing along through life
In this tattered ship of mine
Been rocked and tossed about
        But
It's still in tact
        And
Stronger then ever

Just going with the flow

Seen some big waves
It came crashing hard
Tried to avoid it
But, my ship couldn't turn fast enough
Just thankful it didn't sink this ship of mine

See God smiling on me
And as I just float along this sea
I look up and smile back
Winking my eye
And whispering
Thank you God for watching over me

Just going with the flow

I Made It

Through the storms of life
And though the billows did roar
I can look back over my life and say

I MADE IT

Was it easy?
Can't say it was
   But
I can say I have no regrets
If it wasn't for what I been through
How would I have made it to here and now?

I am much wiser now
My character has been tried and proved
When one says my name they think

True friend
Survivor
Mother
Sister
Daughter
Fighter
Counselor

Though I have days when I feel weak
Those are the days I have to look to you
For my strength comes from you up above
For when I am weak
Then you make me strong

I MADE IT

I'm wiser now
I'm stronger now
All because you never gave up on me

I never would have made it without you
I would have lost my mind so many times
If you weren't there to step in right in the nick of time

I MADE IT

You believed in me when I no longer believed in myself
Esteem so low you helped me to really love myself

I MADE IT

I fell so many times
    But
Yet and still

You choose to love me in spite it all

You gave me comfort on those comfortless nights
You wiped my tears late at night
When I tried to hide that I was crying
You mended my broken heart
You were the best friend
That proved to be
The true friend that I needed

I MADE IT

Through the struggles
Through the heart ache and pain
You stood by me and helped me walk this walk

Lord I thank you
For I made it

I would have never made it
If it wasn't for your mercy and your grace

Yep!

A sinner saved by grace
You're still married to me
Sorry for all the times I let you down
No matter what
I love you
With my whole heart
And now I can truly say
I MADE IT

I Am Here for You

I don't ask God to move my mountains
But instead I pray for the strength to climb over them
Through all the things I been through
I still have to thank God for seeing me through
And believe he will always get me through

My life experiences are what made me wiser
Made me stronger, that even when I wanted to give up
He gave me hope to live a little longer

I have to know it's not about me it's much bigger then me
My experiences is to help someone else with a similar past

That girl struggling with low self esteem,
To let her know she will get her esteem back
To the girl being raped by a man she called her boyfriend and trusted
That girl trying to commit suicide over and over again
To that girl that turned to alcohol and weed to escape her reality
I need to let her know trouble don't last always
From being in emotional, physical and verbal abusive relationships
To the woman that risked her life helping to transport
Thinking she is holding down her man
To the girl that had a child out of wedlock
To the girl that loved and lost
To the woman that had the love of her life go out and have a baby with another
To the woman that married for all the wrong reasons
To the woman that has become a single mother
To the woman that was hurt so deep by so many people

There are just so many things to name
So instead of crying about what I been through I take it all as a learning experience
Through my words hopefully I can help make a burden lighter
So I can let someone know I truly do understand
To help wipe some tears
And
Give back hope to those girls that think they are lost and can't live any longer
Let them know I am here if for nothing else to just be your shoulder
Because I truly do understand
I have to let her know whoever she is that she will eventually get stronger
And overcome all the demons of her past
And to let her know she can still have a brighter tomorrow
Be strong my sisters trouble really doesn't last always
Take the bad and make it good to become a better you!!!
If I did it so can you...........

10

A Better Me

She says she wants to be like me
So she imitates me
Kind of like a mini me

But
I tell her
No!

I need you to be a better me

Take my positives and you enhance on them
See my faults
And run from them
Pay attention to my negatives
So for you it can be the opposite

Her temper rages like mine
And
She has no patience
Easily frustrated
So she's quick to act out
If things don't go the way she likes

I keep schooling her
I keep checking her
Need her to get a handle on her temper
Learn to have patience
So by time she reaches a certain age
She would have already mastered herself

Don't want her like me
I need her to be a better me

For at this stage in the game
I have zero tolerance
And
No patience
And
My temper explodes
With no warning
Cutting through anyone in ear shot
And
In that moment
I'm capable of just about anything

Don't want that for her
So I need her to become better than me
Learn to always be in control
And
Not let people
Or situations
Control her

She tries to make me laugh
Because
She see's I'm not myself
It's cute really
Her trying to get me out my funk
But only when I'm in that mood

But I wish sometimes
She would pay attention
Sometimes I just need her to be quiet
My mood does shift
So I need her to flow with me
If we are to remain in the same house

I need her to toughen up
Because
Life will throw her some blows
She gotta understand
In this life
People will always let you down

I need her to be independent from now
Understanding
That she doesn't need a man
Get her head right
Staying focused
I need her to be all that I couldn't be
And reach that place she desires to be

I need her to know
She has to say what she means
And means what she says
It's called having integrity

Be the kind of friend
You require others to be

But
Never put anything past anyone
And trust has to be built
Honor loyalty in people
For that is rare
While she also remains loyal
To what she holds dear

Life lessons I will keep teaching
And yes
She will make her own mistakes
But, I need her to pay attention
Because
There is always someone waiting
To catch you slippin'

I don't want her to be like me
I need her to be a better me
I need her to aspire to be everything I couldn't be

If I Could

If I could
Just turn back
The hands of time
I would go back
&
Re-do my life

The choices I've made
The places I've been
The relationships I had

Yeah I know we shouldn't live with regrets
But there are some things In my past
I would go back and change
If I could just rewind time

Sure they made me who I am today
And of course they made me so much stronger
But
Can't help wonder
Would things have turned out better for me
In the long run

If I could just turn back the hands of time
I would have listened
I would have stayed focused
I wouldn't be in certain positions now
Questioning so many things
Just regretting some choices

I am who I am
No matter what I did or didn't do
No matter what
I may have been through
For I am
Thankful for the wisdom it bestowed

Just wonder at times
How would my life had turned out
If I could actually turn back the hands of time
Then get a do over
Just how cool would that be
&
Being able to go back
With the knowledge you posses now
Man how awesome
If I could just turn it back

Dedication to My Daddy

My daddy
You've been through the storms
You've seen people come and people go
And you often gave more then you received

A strong man you are
Wise and a heart that's pure
You could be stern
But, you always mean good
Compassion that supersedes the norm
And a father to all

Sometimes the road is lonely
And you have no one to turn to
Some days your spirits extremely low
But, you push past what you feel
To make sure your sheep are okay

Often times feeling unappreciated
But, yet you still give
Been betrayed by so many
But, you show what it means to truly forgive

On this day dad
I want you to know
That you are truly appreciated

Not just as a Pastor
Or
A Bishop
But, a father
And a true man of God

Know that you are blessed
And the sacrifices you have made
Have not gone unnoticed
For if you look real good
You will see
Those that are here
Are truly for you
They love and appreciate you
And all that you do

I know at times we may bump heads
I'm a mini you
And when I grow up
I want to be just like you
I soak up your words
Try to apply your teaching
Your strength is remarkable
And that's because God walks with you

I see the sadness deep in your eyes
But, today daddy
And every day of my life
I want you to know
I love you
And I am who I am because of you

God is always with you
He will never forsake you
And he hears your prayers
That resonates from your soul
And he will continue to bless you
And allow you to rise above it all

My Papa
My Daddy
I will always love you

Forever your little girl

I'm Dreaming

I'm dreaming
Of a love
That's true and pure
A love that loves unconditionally
Same way I do

I'm dreaming
    Of
Soft words spoken
    And
Ears to listen

I'm dreaming
Of a love
That transcends space and time
    An
Equal partnership

I'm dreaming
    Of
Friendships pure and solid
And promises made
Never get broken
Where laughter echo's in the air
    And
There's never any despair
Where the sun shines bright
And there's never any dark clouds
in the sky

I'm dreaming
Of peaceful beings
Where only harmony resides
No hate or words of strife
Where animals and humans
Can walk side by side
And never a thought or worry
Of being in harms way

I'm dreaming
 Of
That family I would love to have
That white picket fence
That's all around the yard
The dog and the cat
The big house not too far from the beach
A balcony over looking the garden
And between the four walls
A home with pitter, patter of little feet
Running all around
Where peace permeates the air

I'm dreaming
 Of
Stars that actually grant you wishes
And everyone is tapped into their spirit

I'm dreaming
That no hearts will ever feel pain
Or be broken
Where our past can be transformed
And we get a chance to do it over

I'm dreaming
We never have to utter the words good-bye
For we never have to leave each other

I'm dreaming
Of a world far less complicated
More simple and divine

I'm dreaming
Of a time where everyone can love
Free without restriction
No fear of rejection

I'm dreaming
Of a life
Where there are no murders
No rapes
No molesters
No evil thing to cause corruptions

I'm dreaming
Of a place
Beautiful and free
Where love is love
    And
Everyone feels it
Where we are all
Each others keepers

No room for envy
Or any kind of betrayal
We just love and care
For each other

I'm dreaming
Of a day
Where I can swim out into the ocean
And the sharks and fish
And
All other sea creatures
Can just swim together
What a beautiful sight that would be

I'm dreaming
Of a day
Where there are no more tears
And love ones that past are here
And we have no more fear of dying
For we'll live on for eternity
All being taken up in the rapture
Where we are all are heaven bound

I'm dreaming

In My Daughter's Eyes

In my daughters eyes
I see everything pure
In my daughters eyes
I see hope
In my daughters eyes
I see love
In my daughters eyes
I see me

If I could shield you from the cruelties of this world
To keep you innocent and pure
You know for you I would
And with everything in me I will protect you
But, there will come a day
When you will have to walk your own walk
And learn from your own mistakes
But, I will give you all the arsenals
That I have within me
To help you along the way
So you can learn how to fight your own battles
With me being in your corner
Every step of the way

I been through something's
So that when the day comes
I can bestow my wisdom upon you
Be careful who you give your heart to
And make them prove worthy of your love

Prove its love and not lust
And always stay alert
Side stepping the traps
The devil will place in line

Know that you will have friends that will betray you
And out of ten friends
There might be only two that's true blue
When you find that really good friend
That keeps your secrets
And has your back
You hold and treasure that one dear
Be it male or female
For true friends really are hard to find

Focus on School
Let that be your priority
So you can be that pediatrician you want to be
Always be a leader
And never a follower
You set the pace
And always walk with grace
Remember you're please and thank you's
Because, you were brought up with manners
Carry yourself like a lady at all times
And never let them see you slippin

I pray you laugh often
And hurt less
Remember you have so much strength
You just have to tap into it
Always remember

That no man defines you
In order to receive love
You must first love yourself

So you walk with your head held high with confidence
And let no one break your stride
And if by chance you stumble and fall
Baby girl,
Brush yourself off
And, get back up again

In my daughters eyes
I see promise
In my daughters eyes
I see hope
In my daughters eyes
I see forgiveness
In my daughters eyes
I see love
In my daughters eyes
I see me

Last Night

Last night I read a book
It spoke to my soul
Took me to far away places
The words hypnotized me
Held me

In it I found shelter
In it I found solace
The words engulfed me

Relating to the main character
For she spoke just like me
Her fear
    Her dreams
        Her longing
            Her hurt
Was all to familiar to me

Last night I read a book
That took my breath away
Pulled on my imagination
And it played out in my mind
Scene by scene

She talked of wanting true love
Not just any kind
But, the one that would fit her just right

She talked about the whole push and pull you do
Because, part of you wants
    And
The other part
Scared
So you pull away

I lay there pensive
How could she speak of things
That is a reflection of me

Last night I read a book
And for once
I felt this author understood me

She talked about getting up and moving
And dealing with being alone
For a moment I closed my eyes
Cause I could feel my tears welling up

She touched on places and feelings
That lay in the crevice of ones soul

Last night I read a book
That pulled on emotions
And somewhere between reality
And fantasy
It soothed my soul
It tickled my heart
And the words danced around in my mind
It all made me smile

BSavvy

She asked something
Made me pause
"Could she love herself enough
To let someone else discover
All the love that lies within her?"
A question
I repeated over and over again
Waiting for the answer
To which I had none

Last night I read a book
That I will treasure
And refer to it as priceless
For this Author, Artist, Adventurer, Lonely, Strong woman
Wrote her book with details
Reminiscent of my life

All who she is
All she hopes to be
All she hopes to find
Sounds so much like me

As if she read my mind
Saw my heart
Felt my longing
Knew my pain
Understood my hurt
&
Had the same joy

I loved on the play of words
I was truly blown away
Hopelessly romantic
Or
Am I just
Romantically Hopeless
Is a question I must ask my self

Last night I read a book
That took my breath away
It was like a warm breeze
On a summer night
It did my soul well
She tapped in to me
And for once I felt understood

Last night I read a book
That took my breath away

Make - Up

In the morning she will rise
Feet placed on the floor
She surveys the room

Inhale
        Exhale

She glances the time
And hurries along

Stops in the mirror
Applies her make up

For every stroke of the brush
For every line of the pencil
The foundation she wears
For the gloss that glides across her lips

Her make up
Is her cover up

Hiding the flaws
For she sees imperfection
In what God knew was right

Adds some eye lashes
She wants them long and thick
Hoping it will distract them all
From seeing into her soul
And seeing who she truly is

Her make up
Is her cover up

It helps give her confidence
When she is really lacking
Self confidence
For she is filled with insecurities

At night she washes it all away
Looks in the same mirror
To see a different face

Her true self
Staring her in her face
She is displeased

Her vision tainted
Distorted
    But
Reality is

She's beautiful
Without the make up

        And

In time she will see
She will believe
God makes no mistakes
And she will learn to embrace
And love
Everything about her face

Her eyes are beautiful
Her nose proportioned
To fit just right
Her lips
Luscious and beautiful
Her lashes
Were made
The way they were intended to be
Cheeks round and nice
To fit her face

For she is beautiful
And if no one ever told you
Doesn't matter
You tell YOU
While looking in the same mirror
You are beautiful
Without the make-up

17

May He

I know it's hard right now
Seems the trials won't stop
Seems like the pain
Just won't go away
It seems like the billows
Just keep on rolling
The ocean waves is a bit rocky
Rip tide waves crashing in
Feeling like it's sucking you in
Trying to take you under
As if the sun has hidden its shine
Depression got you bound
The tears just won't seem to stop flowing
Feelings of loneliness has taken hold
No one to turn to
No one to lean on
No one who can possibly understand
Well I can truly say that I identify

But right now this is my prayer for you

May He

Give you strength to ride out your storm
May He hold you in the midst of confusion
May He blow his breath of life upon you when you feel defeated
May He kiss your forehead and remind you that you are loved
May He gently wipe away every one of your tears
May He carry you when your legs get a bit weak

May He hold you when you feel all alone
May He listen carefully to when you speak
May He answer every one of your prayers speedily
May He give you comfort when you feel comfortless
May He send someone to your side when you have reached your breaking point
May He minister to you constantly as you lay in your bed at night
May His soft words into your spirit soothe all your pain and fears away
May He keep you safe when surrounded by your enemies
May He keep your ears blocked from negative speech
May He seal your lips when you feel you are going to say the wrong things
May He bring back your smile
May He give you back your peace
May He restore back your strength
May He give you clarity
May He keep love in your heart so you never turn cold

To the loveless
I pray you find love
To the one that has turned their back on love
I pray your heart won't remain so cold
But, instead one day
Be open and willing to embrace love

Letting go of yesterday
And embracing
Your better tomorrow's

This is my prayer for you
Remember to shake it off
And let the devil take it back

Remember you are Royal Kings and Queens
Princes and Princess
So take your place
And return back to your throne
For you are
And will always be
Someone special
And someone of Royalty

I speak life back into each and every one of you

Live each day as if it was your last
And
Fight hard to keep that which is called your peace of mind

Missing My Muse

I don't have my muse
So it's like my pen is on mute

Searching for words
To paint the pictures
Of what goes on within my soul

Mental block
I'm now experiencing
Want to write
Want to express
But, my pen is on mute

Missing my muse
Because now my creative juices isn't flowing
Words that flowed so easily
Describing how I was feeling
Has now wondered off

Close my eyes
And listen for the words
The words that once echoed in my head
As I quickly went to jot them down
Now I only hear crickets instead

Went from feeling
To now being numb
My muse inspired me
Helped my pen flow

Hate to admit it
    But
I'm missing my muse

Now I Can

Remember when the reflection
I saw was not my friend

Thinking back on many nights
When I was younger
How I avoided facing it
Didn't like who I saw
Nothing about me screamed beauty

Writing words
All over that mirror
Expressing self hate
Thoughts of suicide
Took over

Thanking God
Today
I can now look in that mirror
And admire self

Knowing I am beautiful
Inside and out
Loving my pure heart
Regardless of all the hurt I encountered

Seeing me for the first time
No more veil covering my eyes
For circumstances
        And
Childhood memories

Doesn't define me
It just helped me be who I am today

I see the growth
I love the twinkle in my eye
I love each and every curve

******

Took his words to heart
That I wasn't beautiful
No man would want me
So many words tore me down
That just added to my own self hate

Never appreciated compliments
Just knew they were lying
Just didn't see
What they saw
So I couldn't accept it

Took years to rebuild my self esteem
But
I built my house
Brick by brick
This time with a strong foundation
You can't tell me
I don't know my worth

For now I have self love
Loving my faults and all
Can look in the mirror
And the reflection which is me
Looking back at me
And smile
For I love who I see

Won't let my fears imprison me
Go out and explore the world
Telling all the young women
What it's like to now love yourself
What it's like to now know self worth

Reach for the stars
Let no man tear you down
And regardless of your circumstances
And where you're coming from
Your situation doesn't define you
Love yourself inside and out
Never settle
And learn
How to encourage yourself
And
    That
God is love

Resentment

Resentment builds
From words
Never uttered
Buried
One on top of the other
Slowly but surely
It's bubbling up
Like a volcano about to erupt

Like popping firecrackers
On the fourth of July
One by one they go off
    But
It's not done
Holding back that big one
Trying to suppress it
Push it away

Everyone laughing
Going about their business
Stuck in their own world
Oblivious to what's happening inside you

Then the finale'
The M80
Goes off
It's the big explosion

It rattles the house
Echo's throughout
The roaring
The boom
Everyone looks to find out what happened

So out the blue
It wasn't expected
    But
You knew it was coming
You just couldn't peg the exact moment

Words spewing
You start at A
    And
Keep going
Till you reach Z
Bringing up things
Others long forgotten

You can't stop
It's now a chain reaction
Setting off other explosions
Now it turns into
C40
Dynamite
Blowing it all up

Then the release
Then the smoke clears
You look around to asses the damage
You didn't mean to take it there

But, resentment builds
Now you find
So many others
Has been affected
Tear stained eyes
And the look of hurt plastered
You feel bad

But

Can't say sorry
Not at this moment
Yeah it's late
Should have addressed it all then
But
You can't help always trying to avoid things
Just trying to keep the peace
Living in perfect harmony

Only to find out
Resentment builds
Then the explosion
Leaving pieces of debris
Letting it be known
A bomb just went off
Sound the alarm
We need the emergency crews
Because some lives has now been truly affected

21

Sister, Sister

Sister, sister why are you so down
You smile on the outside
But, I can tell your dying inside

Is it that bad
Because I can feel your pain
Your heart is black and blue
I know
Because I saw it through your eyes
So despite that smile you are wearing
I know it's not real
But only a façade
A put on
Just for the world to see

So shhh!!
Don't you even say a word
Not one word
There isn't anything
I can say or do
To make it all better
So I won't even try
But, I will just say this one thing
I will always be your shoulder
And in me you can confide

Let the tears roll my sister
I'll grab the tissue and give you a hug
Let my embrace be the comfort
Since I know my words isn't enough

My sister, my friend
In me you can always depend
Good times and bad
I will always be by your side
So you go ahead and let it all out
You must believe there will always be a tomorrow

Sisters

Nothing like sisters
Always there to pick you up
There to lend a helping hand

Nothing like sisters
To really feel your pain
Understanding just what you're going through
Because, they been through it as well

No matter how many times you repeat yourself
You still have their undivided attention
Always giving you their shoulder

Nothing like sisters
That notice when you start to change course
They nudge you
And help you get back on track
Reminding you to stay focused
Reminding you that you can do it
Come hell and high water

Nothing like sisters
That even if you show the world your strength
You can always let your guard down with them
Showing that side of weakness

Nothing like sisters
To cry with you
To laugh with you
To encourage you
To celebrate with you
To ride that storm with you

Sisters is not only someone of whom the same blood flows
But
She can also be your real girlfriends
That been down with you
Through thick and thin

My sisters
I love each and every one of them

Never had a birth sister
But
God blessed me with a truck load of them
My confidants
My partners in crime
My shoulders
My ears
My eyes

And sometimes
My sisters cry tears
That I refuse to let down
You hurt me
You hurt them
And
Vice versa

BSavvy

Nothing like a bond among sisters
And I shall always be my sister's keeper
Forever having their back
And ready at all times
With tissue in hand
        Or
That laughter
To get them smiling
And to remind them
We only have one life
So we will live it to its fullest

Never tearing each other down
But, always their to help build each other up

Sisters
You got to love them

23

True Intimacy

I'm looking for true intimacy
For it's more then just a touch
A kiss an embrace
It's more then sex
Passionate love making
Bumping and grinding
More than just screwing
I'm looking for true intimacy

True intimacy for me
Is the ability to see me
I-n-t-i-m-a-c-y
Into me you see
See me, i-n-t-i-m-a-c-y
Intimacy I see
Looking past the façade I show the world
And really knowing me
Knowing that just because I'm smiling
I might still need a hug
It's when I don't have to say a word
You will know just how I feel
By just really knowing me

True intimacy
The ability to see me
We would communicate non-verbally
Because, that is just as deep
When you touch my hand
You will feel my vibrations
And we would connect on a deeper level
When you look into my eyes
You will be able to see my soul
True intimacy for me is you loving me
For me and not who you want me to be
I'm looking for true intimacy

V-Day

Valentine's Day
What is that day really
Cards, Balloons, Teddy Bears, Flowers
And maybe some Jewelry
All year you treated me like dirt
Now because it's V-day you feel obligated
Bump a V-day
I want you to treat me good all year round

Surprise me with flowers on off days
Buy some jewelry just because
Get a card just to express
How much you care throughout the year
So that when V-day rolls around
It's no big deal
Because you took time to care and appreciate me
365 days of the year

V-day what a joke
Dudes that could care less
Come out the wood work
Trying to make up for all the days he was a jerk
And tonight because you spent a little dough
You think I'm suppose to give up the skins

Today I'm my Valentine
Treat myself better than any dude can
And
Can honestly look in the mirror
And say I love who and how I am
Doing it for my darn self
Don't need a man to toss me any bone

So you single girls
Just take yourself out
Enjoy time spent alone
Before a dude comes in
And messes up your mental
Be proud of your self
Because you're doing you
So no one can dictate
A darn thing to you

Cheers it's Valentine's Day
And it's all about YOU!

Slow and Steady

I step………
2 step………

Slow and Steady…………

Come on girl you can do it……….

3 Steps, 4………..

I just want to make it to the finish line
So I can pat myself on the back
And say I did it
I made it
The trials didn't take me under
But, instead I got over

Knees starting to buckle
Come on legs
Don't fail me fail me now
You can't give way
Not just yet

Devil get off my shoulder
For this battle
You haven't won as yet
No white flags waving

Come on girl
Shake it off
Speak that word to yourself
You don't need anyone else right now
Sometimes you just have to encourage yourself
Hear that small voice
Yeah God's right there beside you

Temporary insanity trying to take me
Lord renew my mind
I see the finish line
I just have to make it
My life depends on it

All this weight I'm carrying
Is slowing me down
Feels like I'm slowly loosing focus

Oh man my vision is now getting blurry
Can't stop though
Even though I need some rest
Okay, how about I take a quick break instead

****

Oh thank you Lord!
You came in the nick of time
I almost gave up
I feel the burden getting lighter
I feel a little bit better

Strength being restored
Oh wait!
My vision has gotten clearer
I can now make it the rest of the way

How about I take it slow and steady
No need to rush this race
Just as long as I make it to the finish line
Does it really matter
If I make first place

Think I'll take in the scenery
Enjoy life a little more
Because,
Before it was just passing me by
I'll make it for sure
But,
Slow and steady wins all the time

Taking Some Time for Myself

Taking some time to take care of me
For so long
I put others before myself

Thought I closed the door to love,
But you still crept in
Now I remember why
I vowed never to let anyone in

Have to protect me once again
Putting myself above the rest
If I don't love me then who will

I vow to shed no more tears
Closing the door to love
To take some time
And take care of me
If I don't then who will

Buy myself some flowers
Ask myself out on a date
Say, would you like to catch a flick
Yeah, I think I'll go at eight
Take a vacation
Just for self
Lay out in the sun by the pool
Or the beach sipping on something strong and sweet

Have dinner by candle light
Just me, myself and I
Now that would be fly
Ask myself all those questions
People ask when they want to get to know you
On a deeper level

Yeah I'm done with love
Gonna take sometime to take care of me
If I don't love me then nobody will

I'll admire myself
And bask in my own beauty
Then read some books
To mentally stimulate me
And when you pass by

And wonder what I'm doing
I let you know
I'm just enjoying me............

27

Mid-Day Thoughts

Lessons learning
For ever analyzing
Others
And my own actions and motives

Always soul searching
Finding ways to better me
I'm gonna master me
Before I try and master you

Learn my faults
So I can improve on them
Face my fears
So I can overcome them
Remember my mistakes
So I never make them again

Guard my heart
Till I know he's worthy of it
Tell myself live
And
To not just exist

Be open 2 learn
&
Remain teachable
While passing on the knowledge I acquire

Knowing when to be quiet
And
When to speak
Learning how to fall back
And
Let a man be a man

Wisdom is learned
From experience
&
Common sense
Can take you a long way

Taking in my surroundings
Making mental notes
Won't hold a grudge

But
I will remember everything
That proceeds out your mouth
Don't need anyone to validate me
I'll validate myself
Can't lose control of myself
For then
You have gotten control over me

Wondering can I be with a workaholic
If work always comes first
Understanding love is action
Not just words spoken
&
Time waits for no man
So you gotta keep it moving

Doesn't matter
How you look
I'm more concerned with your heart
Money long or short
Don't matter
Rather know
How you gonna treat me over all
&
The heart does break
But I've learned it actually does mend

28

Drift Away

Slow pulls
Deep inhales
Smoke fills room

Head back
It takes effect
I'm floating
No longer here

Drifting to a place
Far better then reality
Painting pictures
Of how my life should be

Laughter erupts
Because of the silliest thing
Then I pause
I can see clearly now
So I stop to examine you
I see who you really are
With out the veil
No rose colored glasses on

Analyze your steps
Watch your movements
Decipher your tone
See the man behind the disguise
It's all clearer now
Yet and still
I like who I see

Take a sip
Feel the warmth
It's working its way down
Helping me loosen up
I'm free to be me
In all my shine and glory

Watch me move slowly
Dancing sensual
Eyes low and seductive
Got to tease you
Fingers moving slow
My touch sends chills

Up and down your spine
Come dance with me
Let's float away on cloud nine
Come join me on this ride
It's all escapism in its truest form
It takes you where ever you want to go
For right now
Everything seems better then reality

To My Brothers

What happened to my brothers
Think they lost their way
Hoping they will catch themselves
Before it's too late

You say you want a Lady
Not just any woman
Don't you realize
In order to catch
And keep a Lady
You have to first act like a gentleman

Carry yourself with dignity
Walk with pride
Pull your pants up to your waist
It shouldn't be hanging off your behind

Be clean and fresh
Watch how you speak

No

Yo
&
Shorty
&
You know what I'm saying

No, we don't know what you're saying
Articulate yourself
You don't always have to curse

Stop starring
Stop gawKing
Like you never seen a woman

Say hello
Good morning
And
Keep it moving
Mystery is very intriguing

Go back to basics
With some
Please
Thank you
&
You're welcome

Try opening up some doors
Pulling out some chairs
Knowing what she wants
So you can order for her

Take the focus off of you
And listen
So you can understand her better

Treat her with Respect
And guaranteed
She'll give it back

If you want to be treated like a King
Then act like royalty
So you can begat a Queen

Show we can trust you
For if we trust you
Then we will submit
And
Allow you that place as the head

Whatever you do
Do it with pride
You don't have to be rich and famous
To turn heads
It's in the swagger
It's the confidence
Not,
Arrogance
It's being able to carry your self
With self respect

Show her chivalry isn't dead
&
Remember
Whatever you start you must finish
So if you started off with flowers
And romance

Please don't stop

You treat a woman like a Queen
Trust me
She will treat you like a King

&
Don't forget
To listen
That's the key

Try to get to know that little girl in her
Then
Love that little girl in her
In doing that
You will get to know and understand
That woman you are with now

Let her know you are trustworthy
And you will love her no matter what
Let her feel protected

And if you love that little girl within in her
The woman won't leave you
But
In return
She'll love the boy within the King

LOVE

30

Expect the Unexpected

I saw him starring
Watched him coming
Had to put my grown woman on
Can't let him know
The nervous feelings
I'm feeling inside

He speaks
I blush
Turn my head
To avoid eye contact

Something about the way he speaks
Grabs my attention
Had no choice
But to give him eye contact

It was a moment
Where time stood still
I was lost in his eyes
He spoke to my soul
And my heart said yes

Nervousness fades
Feelings of familiarity take over
He has me bellowing laughter
Like no other
Dang, this man is one of a kind

Draws me in
I like this feeling
I'm feeling
Think cupid just flew by
Shot me with his arrow
Got hit by the love bug
I think I wanna walk by his side

31

Loving You

Loving you is like loving me
For you are an extension of me

When I hold your hand
I'm feeling my touch
When I see you smile
I see myself smile
For you are the other half of me

When I cry
It's your tears
That trickle down my face
Because,
We are connected
You and I

I love me
So
Therefore
I love you

When you feel down
I pick it up
Because
That's the kind of bond we share

When you comfort me
You're really comforting you
I'm that mirror
Reflecting you

When we made love
We became one
The Yang and Yin
They need each other

You make up
For where I come short
We compliment each other
&
When you feel hurt
I feel the pain
So I help you heal
In reality
I'm healing me

God broke the mold
When he made you
For he made you just for me
And
Me for you

So understanding me
Is me understanding you
Not at all complicated

We'll travel time and space
Lifetime
After
Lifetime
Just to remain by each others side

And

When you pass over
I'll surely follow
For my heart beats your rhythm
&
When I'm not near you
I lose my balance
Because
You keep me standing

The light we emanate
When we're together
It's blinding for the average person
But
They admire us all the same

That's just how deep our love runs

32

Make Love to Me

Late night kisses
That traces
The outline of my curves

Whispers of I love you
Softly in my ear
While pulling me near

Penetration slow
Love making passionate
Taking me on trips
While our bodies merging

I see glimpses of heaven
I'm transported
Between dimensions
Can I just remain here
Where I'm free and uninhibited

Feeling the energy from you
Surge through me
Shooting up my spine
I'm reaching my peak
Climaxing
Bodies moving in-sync
Heartbeats match in rhythm

Head tossed back
I'm exhaling
Releasing all
That's pent up in me

Breathing out
My daily frustrations
You're releasing tension
Built up
That needed escaping

Look at me
With eyes of pure admiration
Love me
Treasure me
But not just because
Of the warmth between my thighs

Let me know I do more for you
Then just satisfy your sexual craving
Love me pure
Love me whole
Take me and always keep me near
Give me the type of intimacy I'm craving
Which is more than physical satisfaction

Touch my heart
Reach my soul
Let me in
I want to go
Where no woman has gone before
I want to stay there
Where you never trusted enough
To believe that's truly where they wanted to reach

I want you to make love to me
Not just physically
But
Emotionally
Mentally
Physically
And
Spiritually
I wanna experience true intimacy with you
I wanna go to other dimensions daily
Because
We take each other beyond
What is considered the norm

When we make love
I want it to be a mind
Body and soul interaction
Where I truly feel you
And you me

Mesh into me
As we intertwine sexually
So we grow on all levels consciously
Fully becoming one

33

Whispers

I can hear the faint whispers of love
Calling my name
Every where I go it's there

I try to loose it
I try to confuse it
I try to hide from it
    But
It's always there
Whispering in my ear
It's trying with all it's might
To win my heart
With words so endearing
Trying to pull on my heart strings

The whispers so soft and sweet
    But
I try to close my ears
I try to block my heart
So if cupid shoots his arrow
It will surely miss the mark

    But

I wonder if it hears my heart
Perhaps it saw past the façade
And recognized just what I want
Doesn't it realize
Fear has a tight grip around my heart
Maybe if I say the opposite of what I mean

Act like I could care less
Would it then shut up
And leave me alone
But,
The whispers it's making me melt

Love oh so beautiful and sweet
Just why have you choosen me
Can you tell I need love over all?

So I decide to bargain with it
See if we can meet in the middle

I'll let you love me
If you give me security
I'll let you love me
If we can keep it light
But yet still deep
I'll let you love me
If you protect me
I'll let you love me
If you can prove
Just how true your love is
Then I'll give in

I have to warn you
I love hard
And it can be scary
So are you sure
You want to win my heart?

The whispers
Still in my ear
Sucking me in
Knowing just what to say
To melt this cold heart of mine

I see the trees blowing
Sun shining so bright
The breeze so warm and inviting
Are you giving me a sign?
That love will be right this time
If that's the case
Then I'll submit to your whispers
Letting cupid reach me this time

Then finally admit
The whispers of love
Has finally won my heart

34

Summer Days

Summer days
Basking in the sun
The warmth touching your skin
Skies crystal clear
Flowers that blossomed
Blue waters glistening
Harmony from the birds singing

Long walks
Deep thoughts
Slow breaths

Cold drinks
Melodic sounds soothing
Breeze blowing
Lovers playing

Night falls
Stars twinkling
Silence echoing
Bodies touching
Lips kissing
Eyes mesmerizing
Love felt

35

Pen for Me

Write lines that describe
You and me
Let your words touch me
Emotionally
Write the words
So I can feel
The love you have for me
Massage my heart
Stimulate my mind
Let me feel you
Deep in my soul
Make love to me
Poetically
I need mental stimulation
That just radiates
Love and true depth

Pen for me

Let your words
Take me on a trip
Where a smile
Appears unknowingly
Where the beat of my heart
Can't help but skip
Where your words alone
Will transform me

Pen for me

Take me to other dimensions
Visualizing the different plains
You take me on
Grab your paper and pen
And take me to verbal ecstasy
To a verbal heaven
Tantalizing
Teasing
Stimulating my mind
Which then stimulates
Every part of my being

Pen for me

Let your words melt my heart
Help me to once again feel
Pull on my heart strings
Touch emotions that lay dormant
So the tears can fall
To remind me
I am human after all

Pen for me

36

Wish I Could Tell Him

Wish I could tell him
Just what he means to me
Without stuttering
Without sounding silly
Without feeling like
I'm just putting my self out there

Wish I could tell him all of what I truly feel
Could he understand it?
Could he appreciate it?
Could he accept it?
Or would it make him run for the hills

A part of me hopes he truly knows
But, I know there's nothing like really hearing it

Wish I had the right words to express what he does to me
Just how he makes me feel inside

Wish I could tell him just how he changed my life

Wish I could make him believe what I feel is real

Wish I could tell him I want him with me

Maybe if I try and construct words
That could paint the pictures like Picasso
Then maybe he could clearly see
Just how much he moves me

I would paint hues of red for the passion
Yellow for the life he gave back to me
Blue for how deep he makes me feel
Green for how I want us to stay well grounded

I wish I could tell him that he is my ministry
And how I want to constantly minister to him
Cater to him
So he could be the best him he could be
Helping him reach his fullest potential
While all the while knowing
He has me holding him down
Stroking his ego
Then massaging his soul with soothing words of comfort
Wish I could tell him that I love the sound of his voice
It's like harmonious melodies to my eardrums
And with each word spoken he plucks at my heart strings

Wish I could tell him I'm sorry
I'm sorry for all that I've said and done
That just contradicted everything I claim I wanted
Letting him know for some reason
I have a tendency to sabotage my own happiness

Wish I could tell him I just haven't been the same
Needing him to not complete me, but to compliment me
For our two halves definitely made a whole
And we enhanced each other's positives

Wish I could tell him I love him
Over and over again until it fully sinks in
Erasing all doubt
Easing all fear

No more second guessing
No more holding back

Wish I could tell him just how tired I really am
Wish he knew just how much I really needed to lay my head on his chest
While he stroked my hair and brushed it back
Then kissed my forehead
Saying baby it will be alright

Wish I could just tell him

*****

Wish he could tell me

Wish he could tell me just how much he misses me
Wish he could tell me he feels the same way as well

Wish he would write me a poem
Expressing everything he is feeling or ever felt

Just need to know
Just need to hear
That you love me still
Do you forgive me?

Can we now finally move past it?
Can we now just be together?
Wish he could tell me

37

One Day

As I gazed in his eyes
My heart just melted
Looking deep in his eyes
I found myself on a journey
Navigating my way through
Hurt and pain
Utter confusion
Wishing somehow
I could help him heal

My twin soul
The yang to my yin
Wishing somehow
He would just trust me
&
Say what lies beneath the surface
Exposing himself
Knowing that releasing
It's the start to his healing

The answers he may seek
Once he speaks
Will then be revealed
Once hearing himself audibly

The ear to listen
The heart to understand
The empathy
To feel what he feels
That will then make us one

I think we walked this path together
In a past life
We found our way back to each other
So on a deeper level
I just feel
I just know
Everything he will say
I will totally understand
&
I pass no judgments

Hoping one day
He will allow
Himself to be vulnerable
&
Truly let me in
Knowing
I'm not here to hurt him

Emotions while messy
Is what makes us human
And even if you have a weak moment
That doesn't make you a weak person

Sometimes it's okay to cry
To open up and truly admit
I'm hurting

And when that day or night comes
I hope he knows
I will be here

&

When he gets too weak
My shoulders are broad
I will carry him
Until he is able
To once again
Walk on his own
That's what friends are for

38

Beautiful Day

Lost myself in the weather
Wind blowing
Sun shinning

I can use a mental trip
Take that trip to the beach
Lay out on the sand
Letting the ocean soothe my soul
While the breeze caresses my skin

Run to and fro
Playing a lovers game
Of cat and mouse
Running towards the water
Being picked up
&
Held tight
As the wave comes in
Slapping both of us

Laughter then echoes
Filling me with such delight
Love felt
And radiates off my face

Waters glistening
Sea gulls soaring
Hands held tight

Don't let go
I softly whisper
Hearing a soft response
    Never
Not in this life time

39

In the Morning

I can smell his fragrance
It fills my nostrils
His scent fills the air
Feels just like he's right here

I can feel his breath
As if he's right in my face
Leaning in
Getting ready to kiss me

I can feel his embrace
So tight
So secure
Embracing
For seconds
Then minutes
We don't want to let go

I can see his smile
It brightens up this dull room
Brings life back in
Where it was once gloom

I hear him speak
He puts me in a trance
With words that sound like music
To my ears

I can feel him
Slowly caress my body
While I slowly exhale

I can feel the passion
When he kisses me
Then
Makes love to me
It feels so real

We lay for hours
Cuddled up
I can hear him lightly snoring
And this time
It doesn't even bother me
&
For once
I was able
To get a good night's sleep

He is my drug
That puts me to sleep
Feeling content
And He
Settles
My restless spirit

I see it all so vividly
And
I think to myself
What an awesome dream
It felt so real

Then the sun creeps through the blinds
Its morning
Time to rise
    And
As I begin to open my eyes

I couldn't believe it
It wasn't a dream
For this man
The man I was missing
Longing for
Dreaming about

Was in fact here with me
    And,
The whole night
Actually did happen
For this time
It wasn't a dream
So I smiled to myself
Leaned in
    &
Kissed him good morning
For what a good morning it is

My Mr. Sexy
Laying here beside me
Holding me
Just like I envisioned
For so many days

40

His Story

As he went about his day
Disguising his hurt and pain
Been through the storms and back
But still he maintained
Showing confidence as his veneer
Hiding his deep insecurities

Does he make enough
Is he a good father
Is he a good provider
Is he appreciated enough
Would he ever be able to truly love again
Would anyone truly just love him

He laughs out loud
But inside he cries
Always told
Men are not suppose to cry

Surrounded by many
Yet he is still lonely
Feeling incomplete
As if there is a missing piece

Been hurt
Been betrayed
So his trust in others
Has diminished

He has guarded his heart
With a wall so thick
Secretly yearning
For that special love
To break in
Then she came along
And gave him unconditional love
And that was something
He couldn't fathom
For he couldn't understand that
Love isn't supposed to be based on conditions

The bond then grew
The connection unbreakable
A man of control
Now finds himself slowly loosing control
Thinking could she really be
Or
Is she just too good to be true

Side by side they lay
&
She told him her story
He looked deep in her eyes
And couldn't believe
Her story was all too similar to his
Then she started to cry

As she cried
Feeling safe to let the real her show
It was then he realized
He was looking in a mirror
One that reflected back his image
For he saw a bit of him in her

As the tears started to roll
He gently wiped them away
Kissing her forehead
And slowly realizing a change

It was in that moment
Her tears woke up his heart
And he realized
He fell in love

That other half
He secretly yearned for
Was laying right next to him
For she was that missing piece
So now his life can be balanced

In the touch of her skin
In the essence of her being
In the innocence of her smile

He made love to her that night
Giving her all of him
And that night
The two became one
With words spoken
From one soul to the other
Would you marry me
And her soul answered yes

41

Just Maybe

Don't know what it is about you
That won my heart

Could it be your smile
Or
The twinkle in your eye
Or
Could it be your voice
That sends chills up and down my spine

Or
Could it be
Just maybe

The purity I see
When I look into your eyes
Or
How your inner child
Relates to mine

Doesn't matter materially
For even if you were broke
I would still be in love with you
The man

Perhaps, it's the confidence you exude
Or the swagger in your stride

Just maybe
It's the way
You make me feel protected
Every time you're by my side

Just maybe it's your touch
That makes me come alive
That words could never describe

Just maybe
It's your laugh
That matches mine

Or perhaps
It's the way you look at me
Making me feel
Like the prettiest girl around

I'm like that butterfly
That just flies around
And you my love
Are the air that keeps me flying
For when your air touches my wings
I just keep soaring

Your soul
Your eyes
Your smile

Keeps touching this heart of mine
That even if we're miles apart
Still feels like you're here by my side

The strength in your voice
The strength in your arms
The gentleness of your touch
The passion from your lips
Makes me want to say
        I do
Forever and always

Just maybe
It's not just one thing
        But
A combination of plenty
That makes up you as a being
That makes my heart
Continuously skip a beat
You're the reason
Why I love you
How could I not
With all the things you are
        And
The things you do
That just keeps me smiling

42

I Want To

I want to
Wake up beside you
Every morning
See your smile
As I open my eyes

I want to feel your arms
Wrapped around me
Legs intertwined with mine
Body pressed against mine

I want to feel your breath
On the back of my neck
As I lay sleeping

I want to watch you get up
And
Move across the room
Taking it all in
Admiring you from head to toe
With no clothes on

I want to watch us make love
By
Looking at our reflection in the mirror
Admiring how you move
&
How our bodies flow in harmony

I want to travel to far away places
Just to experience
Life beside you

I want to hear your laughter
That then sparks mine

I want to listen intently
When you speak
Soaking up your wisdom
Impressed by your philosophy

I want to greet you with a kiss
As you enter our place of residence
Massage your shoulders
Work out your stress
Remind you
This is our safe haven
I want to make memories with you
I want to forever be with you
In this life
&
The next

I want to kiss away your fears
Quell your anxieties
Make them disappear
Reminding you
That there isn't anything
We can't do
We're unstoppable
Because
We are a team

I want to heal your heart
Break down all defenses
Help you believe
In true love again

I want to build back
What was torn down
Brick by brick
I want to see you soar
Help you feel good outside and in

I want to take that trip with you
As we go back in time
Dealing with your childhood
To figure out the source of your pain

I want you to see yourself
Reflected in my eyes

I want you to open up
Leaving your self vulnerable
So I can nurture and love
That part of you

I want that man you are now
And the man you are to become
We take the halves

    And
Make them whole
Becoming one

I want to love you
Forever and a day
I just wanna spend the rest of my life with you

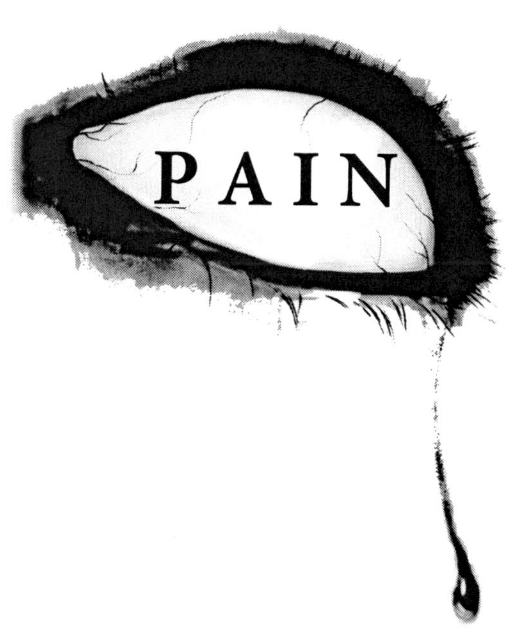
PAIN

Can't Say

Think I said too much
Showed to much
Did to much

When you expose too much
Think that scares them away
For now they know too much

Have to go back to being a mystery
Let him guess how I feel
Keep all my emotions in check
And just not admit how I feel inside

Need to call less
Ignore some calls
Maybe that will get his attention
When he sees
I am not at his beck and call

Let him believe
I don't care at all
I know that's when you get a reaction
Sad, I know
But often times true

Have to make him feel like
He hasn't caught his prey
So he can keep right on chasing me
When in reality he caught me
I just can't tell him so
For then the challenge is over
And I won't be a mystery anymore

For best results don't let them know you fell in love with them

--Let them fall first--

So I'm gonna keep my mouth shut
And not say a word
Instead turn to my pen and paper
To release how he really makes me feel
Knowing where I put my true feelings
He will never read
Never truly know

Sometimes to get the best results from a man
Is to never let him know your heart is his
For he is a hunter on his prowl
He lives for a challenge
Wait to know you fully won him over
To finally reveal just how much you love him

Chasing Pavements

Should I give up
Or should I just keep chasing pavements
Even if it leads no where
Or
Would it be a waste
Even if I knew my place
Should I leave it there

Feels like I've been on this journey forever
Going round and round in circles
Stuck in a bit of déjà vu'
When in reality
It's because I haven't changed my course
Hoping to make the right turn
And it will lead somewhere
But, it only leads me to a dead end street

Back on the path
Feeling confused and tired
Just praying this time the pavement
I'm treading on actually leads to somewhere
But
Starting to feel like
It's all just a nightmare
I can't wake from
Over and over the results are the same
And the pavement I'm on
Is leading me to no where

So I'm asking myself
If this time
I should just give up
Since the results will always be the same
Head spinning
Getting frustrated
Feeling drained
Feeling tired
Heart hurting
Patience running thin
Just ready to throw the towel in
Just maybe
I need to try a different route
And pray it takes me on a different path
And hope my head and my heart will follow

If I give up
Will that make me look weak
If I give up
Will it be known
I didn't really want to
But felt more like I had to
For now I feel my sanity is in jeopardy

Feels like I'm chasing pavements
That is leading to no where
As if I'm on this journey alone
Not a very good feeling
All this time
I guess was just a waste
And I should now start to back peddle

Christina

Chasing pavements even when it leads no where
Hoping for different results what a joke
Who was I kidding
I should have known by now
From the past track record
But starting to get the revelation
It's time to find a different path
For this pavement I'm on
Is obviously leading to no where

Dark Place

He's in a dark place
I'm feeling helpless

Searching frantically for a flash light
To help him find his way
I get in motion
Then stop suddenly

Pondering
Should I let him find his own way out
Or should I show him the light
And
Help him out

Feeling like
It's just him against the world
Not realizing the truth

Perhaps I will run ahead
Show flickers of light
Every now and again
So his curiosity will lead him
Urge him to follow
While all along it's me guiding him
But him making the steps

He's in a dark place

Blowing a fresh wind
In his direction
Sending warmth his way
Fed X some love
And give some comfort
So he knows
He's not alone in this

Remind him of his dream
To know he can't give up
He's a diamond in the rough
A minor set back
But he can't count himself out
He's a fighter
He's in a dark place
Got to help him out

My Prayer

Father God
I'm going through some things
That I can't explain
It's like I'm going through changes
And I keep regressing

Feeling so alone
When I'm surrounded by so many
And when I want people to draw close
I go and push them away

Feeling like a teenager again
Feeling the deep hurt and pain
  And
Tears falling
That I can't contain

Clinging to my daddy
And hugging him so tight
I guess needing his love and his protection
Reassuring me
I will be alright

I sit in his lap
As grown as I am
Just needing to be held
And rocked
Without a word or sound

Life, Love & Pain

I want to cry so bad
And for him
To just wipe away my tears
But I fight against me
And refuse to let the tears roll down my face

Can't verbally explain
What's happening to me
But I went so many years
Ignoring some wounds
That now I think it's back to haunt me

She has risen in search of inner healing
And though
I'm quick to help so many others
I have no idea how to help myself

So Father
Hear my cry
And understand my plea
For I'm not quite sure
What's happening to me
All I know is
I need you to walk this walk with me

Help me see my way through
So I can return to the me
I was before
I don't want to feel the hurt and pain anymore
I need it to go away
So I can laugh once more

Christina

So Father if you hear me
Answer me speedily
Because I'm not quite sure
How much more I can endure
Before temporary insanity
Take a hold of me
This is my prayer
That you come and rescue me

I Should of Neva

I should of neva ignored my gut
    But
Instead listened
When it told me
To just play my position

I should of neva
Let you in
Gave you the keys to my heart
Without you proving worthy first

I should have closed my ears
    And
Opened my eyes
Paid close attention
To see what your actions were

I should have let you work harder
Kept you on the chase
Kept you on your toes
Still trying to figure me out

I should have neva
Let it be known
The day I fell for you
Should have waited
Until you showed not said
How much you cared

Made it too easy
So now
I'm taken for granted
As if I will always be here
With no worries
    Because
I'm always understanding

Problem is

I let you get too comfortable
You think you have me figured out
I guess since you now know
How much I love you
It's not even worth you
Putting forth some effort

I should of watched
I should have paid attention
Just what was the driving force
What was your ulterior motive

Should have ignored your innocent smile
Shrugged off your laughter
Let your charm roll off my shoulders
Ignoring how much of a good man you are
And just
Wait
    Watch
What you would do to prove your love

I should have neva let my guard down
I should have talked less
And listened more

Should have asked for definitions
So we both would have had
A better understanding
Should have stuck to my rules
And
Not let on
Just how much
I really loved you
For
Knowing is power
And I gave you
The power

Thought you could have loved me for me
That was what I believed
So I rode on that tide
But then the wave crashed
&
I went under
And
Nope
You weren't there to save me
But
Instead
You pushed me under

Now looking back
I see
I just should of neva
Gave in that easily

Love Sucks

When they said love hurts
Boy they weren't kidding

It's like he took the knife
Aand started slashing
Bits of flesh hanging
Blood dripping
Then deeper
And deeper
He drove that knife
As I gasped for air
In a state of shock
I didn't even see this one coming

Then the stab to my heart
So quick
And with that last stab
He took out my heart
Then proceeded to stomp on it

You would have thought
I was his arch enemy
When all I wanted
　　And
Tried to do
Was love him unconditionally

As he ranted and raved
The only words to escape my mouth was
Wow!
&
Oh my God!
I was left speechless
With my jaw to the ground

Looking in the mirror
And asking the woman looking back at me
What's wrong with me
What did he see

Then I tell myself
There's nothing wrong with you
Any man would want you
He's just too blind to see

And one day
He will look back and regret
The words that came from his mouth

Hurt people, hurt people
It is truly his loss

But I still can't ignore
How much I loved this man
Left myself vulnerable
All in the name of Love
And this is what I get

"LOVE SUCKS"

Just that quick
This strong woman
Turned weak
Keep shaking my head
Hoping it was just a dream
But the words still echo in my head

I know he's hurt
But damn
You don't get a sista back like that
Assumptions never got anyone any where

He could have talked to me
I would have been happy to clear things up

So here I am feeling
Like the biggest fool
And even more of a fool
Because I still love him

Think tonight I'll down his liquor
Get nice and drunk
Just to numb the pain

I'll worry about tomorrow when it gets here
Tonight I just need to get drunk
So the replay button in my mind
Can just shut off
And I can laugh my hurt away

That's it I give up on Love
Just when I decided to truly love again
This is what I get
A broken heart
And a wasted 2 1/2 years
Because the end results
Wasn't he and I
Till the end of time

Can't believe he didn't even fight for me
But such is life right

Lullaby

As I lay here
Feeling hurt and dejected
Feeling things
I once thought were gone
I find myself rocking back and forth
Hear myself humming a lullaby
Way mommy use to

Hush little baby
Don't you cry

Rock a bye baby
On the tree top

Letting the lullaby
Soothe the child in me
Way mommy use to

Wipe the tears
Hold my self
And whisper
It will be alright

My baby girl walks in
Catches me crying
Asks the question
Mommy, why are you crying?
I never seen you cry
I just looked away and said nothing
I'm not crying
But I really wanted to say
Sweetie I'm not your mother right now
I'm the little girl in your mother
That doesn't have the strength
Your mother posses
I'm the one that feels
All the hurt and pain
So I cry the tears
Your mother doesn't allow to come down

She walks out

I go back to rocking
Stuck in a trance
Of my past
As if I was a deer
Caught up in a head light
I'm regressing
It's all happening again

Hush little baby
Don't say a word

Rock a bye baby
On the tree top

Then I sink
Way down into my bed
Burry my head
And let the tears
Just continue to roll
The little girl in me
Has a lot of pain to release
So I let her
I won't intervene

But, I remind her
Tomorrow
I'm taking back over
I don't like when you feel the pain
I try to keep it away from you
But some how you heard
You saw
And at that moment
You were there
To feel that blow
Sorry

So I'm rocking you now
Singing you a lullaby
To soothe you
And let you know
You will be okay
The same way mommy use too

Hush little baby
Don't say a word
Rock a bye baby
On the tree top
Rest now

Tired of Pretending

I'm tired of tears
&
I don't like pain
I was wondering God
Could you comfort me
Going through something's
I can't even explain

My heart is heavy
&
I'm feeling low again
Need something
To make me feel more secure within

Bottled up all my emotions
Held in all my tears
Tried so hard not to feel the pain
But
Had so many fears

I was wandering God
If you are near
I could use some comfort
&
A friendly ear

Want to release something's
Just don't know where to start
Been abused by so many
Hurt by a lot
Got so many scars
Wish they all could see my heart

Looking for something
To ease my pain
God if you hear me
Please come and rescue me
Feel so drained
Putting up such a front
Wish there was just one person
So I could finally let down my guard

I am so strong
To make it this far
But don't they know
I am still weak inside
Got to thank God
For my different sides
Because that other me
Man she is so tough
She just pushes the pain aside
I mean way deep down inside
Having people thinking she is just fine
She doesn't even cry

Sad part is when I get so close to really breaking down
She shows up again
So no one sees she is really weak inside
So God if you hear me
Please intervene
Because this poor girl is really suffering way deep down within
Got to make her whole again
I long for the continuous laughter and the Joy and peace within
For now it's all just a cover
So no one will know she is really hurting
See what I mean
I've gone to far released too much
She's coming back now
Just so I won't start to cry

Then that leaves me
With so much to carry
That every now and again
I have to resurface
And cry those tears
She wouldn't allow to come down.

Sad part is when I get so close to really breaking down
She shows up again
So no one sees
She is really weak inside
So God if you hear me
Please intervene
Because this poor girl
Is really suffering
Way deep down within
Got to make her whole again

I long for the continuous laughter
And the Joy and peace within
For now it's all just a cover
So no one will know
She is really hurting
See what I mean
I've gone too far
Released too much
She's coming back now
Just so I won't start to cry

Do You See Me?

Silence echoes
Like an orchestra playing
At a symphony
Loneliness engulfs you
Where you walk that fine line
Wavering between
Sanity
&
Insanity

Spinning
Dancing
Laughing
Crying

Mumbling words
Where you ask
&
Answer your own questions

Emotions lay dormant
Draft comes in
Air turns cold

Thoughts intensified
&
You're yearning
For a human touch

Loneliness
It becomes a nightmare
Where your every thought
Is magnified
Even
Painful ones

Perceptions now distorted
Logic and reasoning
Now sounds more like
A babbling fool

Actors & Actresses
Wasn't always born that way
They were created

Scully down
Shades on
Moving around incognito
So you go undetected

Question asked
But never uttered
DO YOU SEE ME
I mean really
SEE ME
Strength of five men
But still
Vulnerable and weak
Like a child
Do you see me

Torn between two worlds
Which one will you choose
    Or
Is that choice
Taken from you

To understand
The nature of a woman
You must listen
Then react

They Say a Man's Not Supposed to Cry

They say a man's not suppose to cry
That's what's wrong with the man today
Living up to this philosophy
So they are constantly dying inside

You can't turn to just anyone
Find that one you trust
Release the things
That has you hostage to hurt

Tapping into
The vulnerable side of you is okay
Know on my bosom
You can surely rest your head
Let the tears fall
So it can soothe the soul
Opening up
Letting your feelings flow
Holding you tight
In your darkest hour
Bringing comfort
With just my embrace

Tonight let's cry together
Take this to another level
Bond on a deeper level
Bringing us closer together
I'll wipe your eyes
    And
You wipe mine
While we hold each other
With candles lit all around
In a tranquil environment
Soft music playing in the background
Both succumbing to vulnerabilities
We never wanted to show another
Tonight can we just comfort each other?

Ignoring all propaganda
Of how men are not suppose to cry
And you just feeling free
To finally release
The way you secretly longed to
No judgments
Just trusting

Your heart
I long to heal
I want us to feel
Taking us on a journey
  Of
Truly
Letting go
  And
Completely loving

The
Good
Bad
And
The ugly

Tonight can we just cry together?
You and I cuddled up next to each other
I wipe your tears
    And
You wipe mine
That to me is love and trust divine

It's okay for men to cry

When A Soul Cries

In the stillness of the night
I can hear screaming
Looking around wondering
Can anyone else hear it
Shake my head a few times
        But
That doesn't stop it
I feel like
I'm loosing my sanity
Where is it coming from
And how can I stop it

Then it hit me
The screaming
Is coming from inside of me
It's my soul crying
But, no one else can hear
But me

I close my eyes
To take a trip within
Search through the subconscious
To dig up some answers
Found out
It's all from emotions
I've suppressed
Feelings of hurt and rage
I never quite vented
I just never released
So now my soul is crying

So while I walk around smiling
Inside I'm slowly dying
Keeping up strength
While suppressing so much pain

The tears were always there
Just never got the chance to flow outwardly
So instead
It turned around
And seeped downward
And flowed into my soul
Overflowing with years
Of hurt and pain
That now It's my soul crying

It makes me
Moan for no reason
I just grunt here and there
But no words escape from me
Sighs of sadness
Escapes my lips
When I was just smiling

Don't think anyone
Will ever understand
What I'm saying
My Soul is Crying

This is what happens
When you turn your pain inward
Instead of releasing it
And letting it truly go

A soul that is screaming
A soul that is hurting

A soul that just endured too much
From outside influence
That the physical body
Just never wanted to deal with

WHEN A SOUL CRIES

He's Gone

I guess he got the memo on me
So I lost him
He just didn't know
My rules of engagement
Never applied to him
Drew me in with his energy
Warm and sweet
So cuddly
Passionate
Yet very aggressive

He's Gone

At one point in time
I fought hard to keep him
It seems now looking back
In hind sight
All that fighting was in vain
Cause now he's gone
The deep connection we had
Is now lost somewhere in the abyss

Woke up one morning
And his voice didn't echo in my head
His smile
I seen so clearly
When I would sleep
Has now faded away
He took his love from me
So I let my heart cry the tears
My eyes refuses to let trickle down

He's Gone

Wonder will he be back
And if the next time
He'll stick around permanently
Or will I not feel quite the same
If and when he came back

I miss his scent
I miss the smooth way
He walked across the room
I just miss

How he just stared at me
For no reason
I miss the laughter
That would always erupt
When we were together

The Yang to my Yin
We were a bunch of paradoxes
But we worked
He was the male version of me
Maybe he flipped the script on me
Played my game
Back on me
Maybe he showed me
Who he thought I wanted to see
Just showed me back
The reflection of me
Perhaps,
I never had his heart
He just played the part
Perhaps he was the biggest actor
And I was his audience

Either way he's gone
So I try
And fight the feeling
I still miss him
I still love him

Hopefully
I'll see him again
In my dreams
Then I could hold him
One last time
And that time
I'll try to engrave him
As a Permanent image in my mind

HE'S GONE

Distance

Not sure what happened
Between then and now
But, the distance between us
Leaves us so far apart

Love resides in my heart
It's in every fiber of my being
I try to remove it
Ignore it
But, yet it remains there still

Perhaps holding on
To the dreams I had
I saw it all in my mind
I fast forward
To take a glimpse of our conclusion
And you were always there
So that makes it hard
For me to erase love
And even though
You make it so hard to love you
I still do

The gaps are so big
And the journey back seems impossible
When your feet hurt
Body weary
From what seems to be
You running around in circles

Everything said
But,
Nothing heard
Just words echoed
To what appears to be
A deaf soul

But

The water runs deep
The love as vast as the ocean
So I still try
Try and tread water
To cross the seas to get to you

They say anything worth having
Is worth fighting for
So I must ask,
Will you give up the chase
And deem it impossible
Because of all that separates us
Or, will you prove your love
And deem me
Worth it all
And fight for me
Same way
I fought so long for you

Or will you let us continue down
Separate paths
Never meeting up finally
Becoming attached

Will you rise above the obstacles
And stay determined
To fight for what you want
Finding your voice
So you can once again
Utter it all

Will you fill in the gaps
Draw us back closer
Finding back your confidence
Because,
I am sure it is still where you left it

The distance left between us
Is just too much
It brings about a deep sadness
One I can't seem to shake
And though confusion
Fills my mind
I know one thing
Remains the same
And it's the fact
That I still love you
And, that will never change

Rude Awakening

Knock, Knock

Is anyone at home?

Think I lost the real me once more

Or was she ever really found?

While being alone
I did some reflecting
Looked deep within myself
Looked way to the core
Realizing
I have emotional baggage with me
Can you imagine
What that did to me?

Here I am thinking
I closed some doors
Never realizing
I never locked them
I just pushed them closed

Didn't want to deal
With the hurt and pain
So I did what I knew best
And that was to push it away
Push it way deep down within me

Was a pro at pretending
Was so use to giving off the façade
That I am just fine
I actually started to believe it
Never took time
To fully realize
I never got rid of the pain
Only masked it
So in reality
I never healed

This is why
I don't trust off the bat
This is why
At times

I believe
I just get sad

This is why
I tried so hard
To not fall in love again

This is why
I dealt with things and people
From the surface only

Understanding

This is why
I keep so many at a distance
Just afraid
If they ever really saw me
And saw my pain

Saw what I really been through
Would they

Could they

Ever

Possibly love me

Or

Would it push them away?

Because dealing with me
And all my emotional baggage
Is just too much for them
To have to end up carrying
All because they fell in love with me

Am I really foolish
For trying to think for them and me?

So busy trying to heal the world
Being everyone's shoulder
Pushing people away
When they tried to return the favor

Then cried some nights
About how
I have no one to turn to

Foolish of me

All because
I feel like
I can't show weakness
Can't leave myself vulnerable
To be hurt again
That whatever I do
I must always remain in control
Of myself
And my emotions

I guess it all makes sense now
To me on so many levels
Why I reject people
Before they can get the chance to reject me

So I guess
I have to start all over again
Learning
To let myself fully heal
Have to take it
One day at a time
Have to learn
That there might be people
Really out there
That will actually
Love me for me

No matter what kind of baggage
I have with me
Needing patience
From those around me
But more importantly
I need to have patience with me

I am grown now
But, the little girl in me
Needs my full attention

For she needs to be set free
So I can finally
Fully
Completely
Be
ME

Acknowledgements

Love

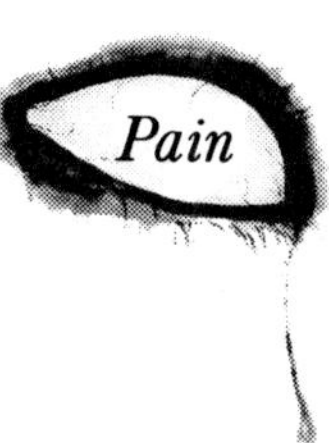

Truly giving God the praise for all he has done for me and continues to do for my family and I, for without him, I am absolutely nothing.

Giving a special thanks to my daughter for being my inspiration, love you baby girl, it's for you I live. A special thanks to my parents Lydia and Michael Frith, my brothers Andre, Sean and Mike Jr. To my sisters, Iria, Billie-Jean, Venisha and Thaniesa for all their support and love and encouragement. Iria, you know the road hasn't been easy, but, I finally made a move Sis, you're next. Love you guys!

A special thanks goes out to my Muse (Jeff) for inspiring me and helping my pen to flow, his continuous support and encouragement is what got me through. Thank you my honey bee for believing in me, I did it thanks to you. We make a good team – The sky is the limit. Love ya!

A special thanks also goes out to my GS (Geo Soul) family, you guys have been my safe haven, my supporters, encouragers, we truly are a family. Thanks for pulling me back when I was ready to pull from the fold and put my pen down. Hugs to you all. Too many to name, but you know who you are. You guys have been my checks and balances. By being among other poets and writers you guys definitely helped me to perfect my craft. You guys rock!!! A big hug to you Kindred -Ga-el you always had my back.

Thank you Vincent for always being there and helping guide me and being a great support system for me, it is truly appreciated.. See, I finally made a move, hugs.

Thanks Blondie, Jessica, Nadine & Val, for all your support and belief in me, Love ya my sisters.

Special thanks, to my sister Rosangela for your continuous support and encouragement throughout the years, you are truly appreciated, Love ya girl...

About the Author

Christina Frith A.k.a. BSavvy started writing from the age of 14. Writing poetry has always been a passion of hers, it was a way for her to release her emotions. It wasn't until five years ago she made her poetry public.

Soon realizing that many people go through the same things, so they could relate. Also realizing that many feel the same things and often times they do not have the words to express how they are feeling, so she writes for herself as well as others. Through her writing she hopes to touch many, comfort many, and inspire many as well.

Life

Pain

Love

Book 2

Excerpt

It Will Pass

Though the storm is raging
&
The billows rolling
Just rest knowing
Your tomorrow is coming

I may not be the strongest
But,
I'll still carry you regardless
Until
You can once again
Carry yourself

Don't let it make you bitter
Just take it as a lesson learned
Never let them see they got to you
Or
Broke you
Even if they did

I pray God heals you
Because
Your pain runs deep
Perhaps
I was sent to you
To help you on your journey

Transitions
&
Transformations
Are never easy
But,
Necessary for your growth

In time
I'm sure it will all make sense
&
Answer your questions
Why
In your head

I pray for healing
For your pain
Calm

In the midst of your storm

Peace
For insanity

Love
For
Hate

Clarity
For
Confusion

Happiness
For
Sadness

And,

Abundance
Where there is lack

Just claim the victory
For you are already an over comer
And,
This battle
By God's grace
Is already won in your favor

So
You lift your head
Rest knowing
This too shall pass

And,

On the sideline
Is me
Storming heaven
On your behalf
&
Cheering you on

I know that you can make it
I know that you will stand
&
Together we stand victorious
For the devil will not win

Smile a while
    And,
Give your face a rest
Your tomorrow is coming
    And,
This will be a thing of the past

Come hold my hand
    For
We'll get through this together

I'll be a true friend indeed
That is really there
Through thick and thin

CPSIA information can be obtained
at www.ICGtesting.com
Printed in the USA
FFOW04n0416200115
10345FF

9 780984 598656